Volume 7

Lost In Michigan
Tales From An Endless Road Trip

◦ETAOIN PUBLISHING ◦
www.etaoinpublishing.com

HURON
PHOTO.COM

Publisher: Etaoin Publishing and Huron Photo LLC
             Saginaw, MI
             www.EtaoinPublishing.com
             www.HuronPhoto.com

Cover Design: Rick Ratell
              Cleaverleaf Design Services
              Midland, MI

Ordering Information:
Books may be ordered from www.LostinMichigan.net

Printed in the United States of America

ISBN 978-1-955474-18-4

Dedicated to Cooper
the best dog ever.

Introduction

I started my Lost In Michigan website in the summer of 2013 as a place to post some of my photos and stories of the interesting locations around the Great Lakes State. Here it is over ten years later, and I am still discovering unique locations and stories to tell. I try to find out of the way places that few people visit and enjoy learning about its history. I am surprised that this is my seventh volume but not surprised that I have explored so many fascinating places in Michigan. It is a beautiful state with a deep and rich history.

The locations in this volume start at the bottom of the state and then work north. Each story is independent of one another. You can read them in any order you wish. I have done my best to give an address that you can use in a GPS to help you find each location. Some places do not have an address, so I have given a description of where they can be found or coordinates for a GPS. Most locations are on public property, but some may be privately owned. Whether they are public or private, they may not be open to visitors, or they may only be open at scheduled times. Most places can be seen from public roads. I don't trespass, and I advise anyone against it. Please be respectful to the places you visit. I hope after reading this book you will take an interest in traveling the back roads of Michigan and see what you can find.

Contents

Chapter One
Southern Lower Peninsula

Chapter 2
Central Lower Peninsula

Chapter 3
Northern Lower Peninsula

Chapter 4
Upper Peninsula

Chapter One
Southern Lower Peninsula

Sam Hill

Location:
139 W Mansion Street
Marshall, MI 49068

You have probably heard the phrase "What in the Sam Hill". It is a euphemism for what in the hell or other possible curse words. Interestingly, Sam Hill was a real person who lived in Michigan. The origin of the saying is

2

unknown, but a possible theory is regarding Samuel W. Hill, who was a surveyor who helped establish the boundary line between Wisconsin and the Upper Peninsula. Hill was a geologist, surveyor, and mining engineer who moved to the Keweenaw Peninsula area where he platted the village of Hancock and worked with several copper mines in the region. He was well respected in copper country for his skills and kindness in helping the community. Hill was also known to use foul language, and when stories were told about him, his name was used in place of curse words, and that is how his name supposedly became a euphemism for swear words.

Hill was twice elected to the state legislature and retired to this house in Marshall in 1875 where he died in 1889. The home is now used as a doctor's office. A historical marker for Sam Hill stands next to it and gives a little info about the man, but does not mention his propensity for swearing.

Franklin Church Munchkin Land

Location:
Intersection of Franklin Rd. and
Frost Rd. near Berrien Center.
GPS Coordinates
41.970975, -86.223927

This cute little white and green church stands in southwestern Michigan a few miles east of Eau Claire. Over the door are the words Franklin Church EST 1854. Next to the church is an old cemetery. Listed as the Franklin Cemetery, it is also known to locals as Munchkin

4

Land. It got the nickname because rumor has it that many people have seen the ghosts of children in the old graveyard.

I have read the story on several sites on the internet. In the late 1800s, the minister at the church murdered two young girls and burned their bodies in the woods behind the church. After being found out, the minister hung himself in the bell tower of the church. I am not sure if the old church is still used for weekly services, but I have seen some old photos of it before it was restored. It looked rather dilapidated, and that is when I assume the ghost stories started being told. In recent years, the old historic building has been restored. The cemetery is a peaceful one with several old tombstones and is an interesting place to visit if you like old graveyards. If you do visit, please be respectful and follow the posted rules.

Treadwell House

Location:
4402 S Meridian Rd.
Hudson, MI 49247

An ornate brick two-story house stands near the southern Michigan town of Hudson as a reminder of the man who built it and his demise. Hudson businessman and banker William Treadwell began construction of this magnificent house in 1862, but he never got the chance to live in the

6

house. William was raised in the town of Hudson and worked at the People's State Bank. In 1859, with capital from his father, he purchased the bank and managed it. A few years later, he was accused of embezzling over 60,000 dollars from the bank and absconded with the money in a suitcase. Weeks after he disappeared, he was captured in Ohio. He was tried and convicted, and on the day of his sentencing, he escaped from jail with the help of an accomplice. The accomplice later murdered Treadwell for the money in his pocket, and Treadwell's body was found in the woods two weeks later. The house William had started constructing was never completed in time for him to live in it since he was apprehended for his crimes. I see a lot of beautiful old houses but not many with a story attached to it such as the Treadwell house.

The house still stands today and is privately owned. The house was designated a Michigan State Historic Site and listed on the National Register of Historic Places in 1974.

> Please note the house is privately owned. You can see it from the road, but please be respectful of the owners.

Parker Mill

Location:
4650 Geddes Rd.
Ann Arbor, MI 48105

The Parker Mill County Park is situated between Ann Arbor and Ypsilanti. There you will find the old Parker Mill. The grist mill was built by William Parker in 1873 on the remains of an old sawmill built by Robert Fleming. Parker ground wheat, buckwheat and corn, and people came to his mill to have their crops ground. Parker also built a cider house next to the mill where he pressed apples and made cider and vinegar, which he sold in local general stores.

After William died, the mill was operated by his son and grandson until the 1960s. After the mill closed, it was purchased along with the land along the creek to create the county park. The mill still stands for visitors to see how grain was milled over a century ago and is open on the weekends in autumn.

A trail takes hikers along the Fleming Creek to enjoy a bit of nature. A paved path connects Parker Mill County Park to the city of Ann Arbor's Gallup Park.

First Women's Club

Location:
333 S Park St.
Kalamazoo, MI 49007

The Ladies' Library Association of Kalamazoo officially incorporated in 1852, and it was the first women's club organized in Michigan and the third organized in the

United States. Its purpose was to promote the cause of equal education for women. The organization built this building in downtown Kalamazoo in 1879, and it was the first building in the nation erected for use as a women's club.

When the club started, yearly subscriptions cost fifty cents and were available to both men and women; however, only women could be members of the organization. In addition to creating Kalamazoo's first lending library, the LLA activities have included advocating for the right for women to vote, the creation of day nurseries for working mothers, founding Kalamazoo's first art club, and establishing a community education program for women.

The Real McCoy

Location:
The Sign stands in Library Park
next to the Library
229 W Michigan Ave.
Ypsilanti, MI 48197

In 1844, Elijah McCoy was born in 1844 Ontario Canada. His parents George and Mildred were former slaves who escaped using the underground railroad through Detroit. At the age of fifteen, Elijah went to Scotland and studied at the University of Edinburgh and was certified as a mechanical engineer. He moved back to the United States and settled in the city of Ypsilanti. The only work he could find was as a fireman and oiler for the Michigan Central Railroad.

With his knowledge of mechanics, he began engineering devices to self lubricate steam engines. The automatic lubricators became popular with railroads because they minimized the need for locomotives to stop and be hand lubricated. McCoy had several patents on the devices he engineered, but like many good products, imitators began

manufacturing inferior knock offs. Railroad engineers knew the McCoy lubricators were the best and began asking if the locomotives had "the real McCoys" on the trains.

McCoy continued to invent products mostly related to steam engines and obtained fifty-seven patents. In 1929, he died at the Eloise Infirmary in Westland at the age of 85 from complications and injuries of an automobile accident seven years earlier. Steam engines and lubricators have been replaced with modern technology, but the phrase still remains as slang for "the real thing" and is a reminder of a great African-American engineer that was the real McCoy.

A historical marker stands in a small park next to the library in downtown Ypsilanti near the spot where Elijah McCoy once had a shop. In 2001, McCoy was inducted into the National Inventors Hall of Fame in Alexandria, Virginia.

River Raisin Battlefield

 Location:
The Visitor's Center is located at
333 N Dixie Hwy.
Monroe, MI 48162

On the corner of Elm and Dixie Highway between downtown Monroe and I-75, a 15-star American Flag waves over the historic River Raisin Battlefield in Monroe. It commemorates the Battles of Frenchtown and the deadliest battle in Michigan's history.

The first battle was fought in January 1813, when a small American force under the command of Colonel William Lewis attacked a British and Native American force at Frenchtown. The Americans were victorious, driving the British and Native Americans from the town.

The British and Native Americans retaliated four days later. Many of the Americans were inexperienced troops from Kentucky, and they were ill-prepared and unable to retreat. Of the thousand American soldiers, 397 were killed and 547 were taken prisoner. The prisoners were marched to Detroit, and those too weak to walk were killed.

The battleground officially began operation as a national park on October 22, 2010, and is the only national battlefield marking a site of the War of 1812. A newly constructed visitor's center is open seven days a week. The NPS plans to construct a recreation of the Frenchtown settlement in the next ten to fifteen years.

The battlefield is along the River Raisin Heritage Trail that leads to the nearby Sterling State Park and downtown Monroe. It is a paved non-motorized multi-use path for bikers and walkers to explore the area.

The Newton House and the Forest

Location:
20689 Marcellus Hwy.
Decatur, MI 49045

The small community of Volinia is located about ten miles northeast of Dowagiac in the southwestern corner of the Lower Peninsula. A few miles west of the town is a large white two-story Italianate style house that stands in the Fred Russ Experimental Forest. Known as the Newton House, it was built in the 1860s for state legislator George Newton. George was the son of Colonel James Newton, who served in the war of 1812 and was a member of the 1835 Michigan Constitutional Convention.

In 1931, Fred Russ purchased the house and the surrounding 580 acre parcel of timberland. In 1942, he gifted the land to Michigan State University, which created the Fred Russ Experimental Forest in his honor. The University Forestry School uses it to conduct long-term research on Christmas tree seed production and other projects aimed at preserving Michigan forests.

I could not find out any information on Fred Russ, but it was an incredible gift he gave to MSU and Michigan. The university also leased a portion of the forest to Cass County to create a park where visitors can hike the trails through the forest. The Newton House was restored by the Cass County Historical Commission and is now used as a museum.

The Fred Russ Experimental Forest is where maple trees are tapped for the sap to create Spartan Pure Maple Syrup sold at MSU stores.

The Nike Base

Location:
Old Woodall Rd.
Shelby Township, MI 48317
42.647690, -83.060526

River Bend Park in Utica sits along the Clinton River. It has baseball fields, soccer fields and a shooting range. Near the middle of the park is a historical marker that stands as a reminder of what the park used to be. The property was originally developed in 1955 by the military as a Nike missile base. Fifteen such bases were placed around Detroit to defend the city in an attack. Ajax missiles were used to shoot down any enemy aircraft that could drop a nuclear bomb on the city.

By the 1970s, the Soviets had intercontinental ballistic missiles and the Nike bases were not capable of shooting them down. In 1974, the bases were deactivated. The missile silos were filled in, and the buildings were demolished. The property was given to the Michigan DNR. All that remains of the old base are a few foundations from the buildings and one small building that is being used as a storage shed.

A deactivated Atlas missile stands in Young Patriot Park in Riverview, Michigan. The park was part of another deactivated Nike missile base.

Kirk in the Hills

Location:
1340 W Long Lake Rd.
Bloomfield Twp, MI 48302

Standing near the shoreline of Island Lake in Bloomfield
Hills is a church that looks like something from medieval
England. Called Kirk in the Hills, it is modeled after
Scotland's Melrose Abbey. Colonel Edwin S. George, a
Detroit businessman whose gift of his home and estate in

1947, made the Kirk possible. The cornerstone for the church was laid in 1951, the same year Colonel George died. His remains are entombed under the narthex of the Kirk's sanctuary. The architectural firm of George D. Mason completed the church based on preliminary designs by Wirt Rowland. George Mason designed several of Michigan's iconic buildings, including the Grand Hotel on Mackinac Island.

It was almost a decade before services could be held in the church. During construction, a fire destroyed the roof and delayed completion of the church. The first service was held in November 1958.

The tower on the church is named the Tower of the Apostles, and it contains the world's largest carillon in the number of bells at seventy-seven. A carillon is a set of bells in a tower, played using a keyboard or by an automatic mechanism similar to a piano roll. During the summer months, the church holds a concert series featuring artist's performances on the bells.

Kirk is the Scottish word for "church".

Land Office

Location:
113 W Chicago Rd,
White Pigeon, MI 49099

This white building with green trim stands in downtown White Pigeon near the southern Michigan border. It is one of the oldest buildings in the state. The Treaty of Chicago was signed in 1821 by the tribes in southwestern

24

Michigan, turning over their lands to the federal government. In 1831, the government opened this office in White Pigeon, one of the largest towns in the western Michigan Territory between Detroit and Chicago on the Sauk Trail, which is now US-2. The office operated between 1831 and 1834, and sold land at $.25 per acre. About 260,000 acres were deeded, including the land that includes Kalamazoo, Grand Rapids and Battle Creek.

The building is now maintained by the St. Joseph County Historical Society, which holds exhibits on surveying the land contracts in the early days of Michigan.

Noahquageshik

Location:
Cressey Rd,
Hickory Corners, MI 49060
42.42795, -85.45738

In a rural area between Plainwell and Battle Creek is the gravesite for Chief Noahquageshik (known as Chief Noonday by Europeans). Marked by a simple wooden sign and a granite marker between a farm field and the road is the final resting place of the great Native

26

American Chief. I wonder how many people have passed by this simple grave site not knowing the history of this remarkable person who died so long ago.

Noonday was the name given to him by Europeans. His real name was Noahquageshik, and in his early years he lived in what is now the Yankee Springs area in southwestern Michigan. Noahquageshik fought alongside Shawnee chief and warrior Tecumseh in 1794 during the Battle of Fallen Timbers near Toledo, Ohio. In the war of 1812, the two leaders fought the Americans in the Battle of the Thames. Tecumseh was killed in this battle, and Noahquageshik inherited his tomahawk and hat.

For several years after the War of 1812, Noahquageshik defended his tribe's land and opposed treaties with the U.S. government. In 1836, the tribe endured a harsh winter and a year-long outbreak of smallpox. After these challenging times, Chief Noonday signed a treaty in which the Ottawa agreed to sell the Grand River lands to the United States in exchange for five-year reservations in west and northwest Michigan.

Noahquageshik died in 1855, and he was laid to rest in this spot in southwestern Michigan. I am sure at the time it was a forest or rolling meadows and a beautiful spot. Over the years and decades, the land has been transformed into farmland and roads for motorists. Today, it seems strange and unfitting to me for a great tribal leader to be buried in such a mundane place, next to a road with a simple wooden marker. The Chief Noonday Outdoor Center was named in his honor and is located in Yankee Springs Township in the region where he spent his youth.

> A bronze statue of Noahquageshik stands on Grand Valley State University's campus in downtown Grand Rapids.

Jail Foundation

Location:
313 N Cass St.
Berrien Springs, MI 49103

In the southwest town of Berrien Springs is a collection
of historic buildings. They include a courthouse, log cabin
and sheriff's residence. The sheriff's house is a two-story
Italianate style brick building that was built in 1870. Next

to the sheriff's house is an odd-shaped foundation, a reminder of a unique jail that once held prisoners in the southern Michigan town. Built at the same time as the sheriff's residence, back when Berrien Springs was the county seat, the jail's unique design was inspired by Auburn, New York, which pioneered the humane treatment of prisoners.

The building was a square brick building, but inside the 24 jail cells (16 on the first floor and 8 on the second) were arranged in a circle. It was two stories tall and in the center was a sky light and a vent for lighting and fresh air. The cells on the upper floor were large and were used for holding female prisoners. The bottom floor was where male prisoners were held. The cells seemed small, but the jail never held long-term prisoners. The cells had two doors. The outside doors were metal bars and the inside doors were solid steel. In the center of the jail was a wash tub and a cistern to hold water. In 1883, eight prisoners removed the wash tub and pumped out the cistern. They tunneled out under the jail and escaped. They were quickly captured, but it brought a lot of attention to the jail, and many curious people came to see the hole where the prisoners escaped from.

After the county seat moved to St. Joseph in 1894, the jail was left abandoned. In 1916, it was demolished, and over time the sheriff's residence was turned into apartments. Now it is part of the Courthouse Square maintained by the Berrien County Historical Association. A replica foundation and cells stand as a reminder of the unique jail that once stood in Berrien Springs.

Parady Park

Location:
208 Main St.
Nashville, MI 49073

Parady Park sits in downtown Nashville, Michigan, located somewhat between Lansing and Kalamazoo. The park is named in honor of Emory Parady. He was born in New York in 1844 and was one of twenty-seven men from the 16th New York Cavalry Regiment who rode with the two detectives tracking John Wilkes Booth after the assassination of President Abraham Lincoln. On April 26, the patrol found Booth hiding at a Virginia farm. Two days later a fire was started to force Booth from the barn. During the fire, one of the men shot Booth in the neck. He was pulled from the barn and died a few hours later.

In 1866, Parady received a $1,365.84 reward for his role in Booth's capture. Parady settled in Nashville with his wife and son in 1870 and worked for many years as a cobbler. He served as justice of the peace in 1879 and was president of the village council from 1883 to 1884. Parady also worked as the village postmaster for several years. He and his wife raised five children in Nashville, but in 1906, Parady and his family moved to Portland, Oregon, where he lived until his death in 1924.

Chapter Two
Central Lower Peninsula

Spring Grove

Location:
1800 Greenly St.
Grandville, MI 49418

Southwest of Grand Rapids, near Jamestown, is Spring
Grove Park. The sixteen-acre park is a county park that
has a stream flowing through it fed by a natural spring in
the back of the park. Crystal clear water bubbles up

through the ground into a pool of water surrounded by stones. It reminded me of a small version of Kitch-iti-kipi at Palms Book State Park in the Upper Peninsula. If you are looking for a nice place for a stroll or stop for a picnic, check out the little park in Southwest Michigan.

The park is open from April to October and closed during the winter months.

Whites Bridge

Location:
White's Bridge Road near Smyrna
43.014590, -85.297871

Located between Greenville and Smyrna, Whites Bridge crosses over the Flat River south of Smyrna. The covered wooden bridge is named for the White family that settled in the area. Levi T. White built the first bridge to cross the river in 1840. It was made using logs and needed to be replaced in 1856. The second bridge was destroyed by an ice jam. The local citizens needed a sturdy bridge and hired bridge builder Jared N. Bresee to build a new covered bridge for a sum of $1700. Constructed in 1867, Whites Bridge stood for generations and has withstood the harsh Michigan weather for decades.

The bridge was completely incinerated by a fire set by an arsonist on July 7, 2013. With grants from the state of Michigan and fundraising efforts by Whites Bridge Historical Society, $475,000 was used to construct a replica of the covered bridge. This was a lot more money than was needed to construct the original one nearly a century and a half ago. The new bridge was completed and opened to traffic in 2020. It may not be the original, but it is a beautiful bridge and a joy to drive across it.

Jared N. Bresee also constructed the nearby Fallasburg Covered Bridge.

Clare County Poor Farm

Location:
980 Old County Farm St.
Harrison, MI 48625

South of Harrison is a stairway that leads to a small field surrounded by stone pillars and metal fencing. It is a cemetery and all that remains of the old Clare County Poor Farm. There are no headstones or markers, but it is believed that about 100 bodies are buried in the cemetery.

They were former residents of the poor farm and died while living there.

The first poor farm in Clare County was built in 1871 in Grant Township near the city of Clare. When the county seat was moved to Harrison in 1879, a new poor farm was constructed in Hayes Township. In 1912, a new poor farm was constructed just south of the town of Harrison and renamed the Clare County Infirmary. It closed in 1945 and burned down a few years later. The area that the residents farmed is now the landfill.

Poor farms were working farms and a place to live for destitute people. The residents who were able to work were required to do so, and the elderly and disabled were cared for while living at the farm. It was a time before social welfare programs and nursing homes; at one time almost every county in Michigan had one.

The Big Weather Vane

Location:
5401 Eagleson Rd.
Gladwin, MI 48624
44.0163093, -84.583955

Driving through the countryside near Gladwin, you will probably pass some Amish people traveling in a buggy pulled by a horse. That would not be that uncommon in the farmland northwest of Gladwin, but you may also see a massive arrow on a pole that has an antique tractor and

42

plow on it. Located near the intersection of Bard Road at Eagleson Roads, the weather vane was constructed by a local farmer. It does work and points into the direction of the wind. Around the edge of the farm field where the weather vane stands are old tractors. Some are arranged in whimsical orientations standing on the rear wheels. They remind me of the tractor "cows" in the Pixar movie Cars.

In the west Michigan town of Montague is a weather vane that has claimed to be the largest weather vane in the United States. I am thinking the one in Gladwin is larger. I am not sure which one is officially larger, but both weather vanes in Michigan are impressive and worth a road trip to see.

The Thing in Trufant

Location:
100 E 2nd St.
Trufant, MI 49347

The small town of Trufant is located in the farmland between Greenville and Howard City. In the center of town is a massive thing standing in a park. The enormous tripod made of logs the size of telephone poles was used for pulling stumps. Using ropes and chains, a crew of men

44

used the framework to pull huge stumps left over from the lumberjacks that harvested the timber in the late 1800s. The stumps were lined up along property lines to create "stump fences".

According to the sign in front of the stump puller, it was made in the 1900s and was used to clear farmland in the region. After it was no longer used, Donald and Irene Gustavsen became the owners of this unique piece of history. They displayed it on their property in Six Lakes. After Donald's death in 2000, Irene donated the stump puller to the town of Trufant because it has a Stump Fence Festival every Labor Day weekend.

The town is named for Emery Trufant, who built the first water-powered sawmill in the region in 1872.

The Grice House

Location:
N Lakeshore Rd.
Harbor Beach, MI 48441

This beautiful fieldstone house stands along M-25 north of Harbor Beach in front of the Marina. It was built by James Grice, who came to the Thumb with his five sons and one daughter in the 1860s from England. He worked at a local sawmill and built this house made of timber and fieldstone. The house survived the great fire of 1881 and remained in the family until the 1960s, when it was acquired by the city of Harbor Beach.

After the city took ownership of the home, volunteers converted it into a history museum. Many local citizens donated artifacts to display in the home. The kitchen, living room and bedroom are the way they would have been when the home was first constructed. The other rooms display military and marine artifacts, including the fresnel lens that was removed from the Harbor Beach Lighthouse in the 1980s.

Next to the house is the Adams School House, which was built in 1920 and moved to its current location in 1988. Behind the house is the North Park Pavilion, which once stood across the street before it was moved in 2015.

First Pro Football Game

Location:
7002 M-21
Ovid, MI 48866

A few miles west of Ovid along M-21 is the town of Shepherdsville, or at least what remains of it. The town was named for William Shepherd, who first homesteaded the land in 1866. The town grew in population after the railroad came through and built a depot. Unfortunately, a series of fires destroyed most of the town, and instead of rebuilding, many of the citizens moved away.

One of Michigan's most notable events took place in the forgotten town. Next to M-21 is a brick marker that stands next to a party store. I am sure many motorists have zoomed past this monument with a sculpture of a football and shoe on top of it and never stopped to read the plaque, which reads, "In the field south of this site on July 4th, 1895 the Michigan Rushers, a local team, played the first professional football game in Michigan, and possibly in the U.S."

The marker was erected in 1995 after the 100th anniversary game was played. During that time period, there were not professional athletes like there are today. Most people thought it was improper to be paid to play sports, so athletes took money or items such as watches in secret. It is believed that the game in Shepherdsville sold tickets and at the end of the game the proceeds were divided among the players, making them early professional athletes.

According to the Pro Football Hall of Fame, the first professional game that was played by the Allegheny Athletic Association football team defeated the Pittsburgh Athletic Club on November 12, 1892. The University of Michigan became the first school west of Pennsylvania to establish a college football team. On May 30, 1879, Michigan beat Racine College 1–0 in a game played in Chicago.

Log Cabin Church

Location:
1030 W Tuscola St.
Frankenmuth, MI 48734
Across from St. Lorenz Church

The town of Frankenmuth at the base of Michigan's Thumb is the most popular tourist destination in Michigan and possibly the Midwest. Thousands of people come to eat a world famous chicken dinner or visit Bronner's Christmas Wonderland. On the west side of town, the steeple for St. Lorenz Church towers over the town of Frankenmuth. An old graveyard sits across the street from the church and is the final resting place of some of the town's earliest residents.

In the back of the graveyard is a building constructed out of logs. It is a recreation of the original log cabin St. Lorenz Church dedicated on Christmas Day in 1846. The original church was built by fifteen German immigrants who came to the area in 1845. The settlers named the "colony" Frankenmuth by combining the name of their home region, Franconia, with mut, the German word for courage. If you visit the popular town and you like old cemeteries, be sure to visit the historic one across from St. Lorenz Church.

The Barn Boat

Location:
3560 Fehner Rd.
Port Austin, MI 48467
43.978691, -83.123428

This odd-looking structure stands a few miles south of Oak Beach between Caseville and Port Austin. Titled CELESTIAL SHIP OF THE NORTH (EMERGENCY ARK), it was created by Detroit artist Scott Hocking. Since the 1990s, he has been creating art installations using abandoned buildings and discarded items such as old boats to create his sculptures.

Constructed on Goretski Family farmland in 2015, the "Barn Boat", as some call it, was created using materials from a collapsed 1890s barn and took three months to build. Hocking was inspired by the story of Noah and his ark when he came up with the concept. It is an odd sight to see, but it is on private property. Because of its massive size, you can get a good view of it from the road.

Not far from the Barn Boat you can also see two other barn artworks *Secret Sky* by Catie Newell, and the *Pigeon Mural* by Hygienic Dress League.

The Worst Environmental Disaster in Michigan

Location:
149 E Crawford
St. Louis, MI 48880

A stone marker stands like a tombstone next to the former train depot in St. Louis, Michigan. The depot now serves as a history museum. The marker once stood in a nearby field, warning people of the contaminated soil from the former Velsicol Chemical plant. It was the site of the worst environmental disaster in Michigan.

In 1973, farmers around Michigan began to notice milk production of their dairy cows had begun to decline. It was not long until the cows stopped eating and their calves died. After researching the illness, the cause was traced back to the animal feed and it was found to contain high levels of polybrominated biphenyl, or PBB, a chemical used as a fire retardant.

A year later, in April 1974, it was discovered that the PBB retardant was mistaken for magnesium oxide, a cattle feed supplement. The two chemicals came from the Velsicol Chemical plant, and the sacks of PBB were sent to the animal feed plants by mistake. 30,000 cattle, 4,500 pigs, 1,500 sheep, 1.5 million chickens were killed and buried in mass graves after the discovery of the mixup. It was a devastating blow to many livestock farmers and forced them into bankruptcy.

Fifty years later, it remains one of the largest environmental disasters in American history. The Velsicol Chemical plant closed down; it was demolished and buried where it stood. The stone maker was placed in its location to warn people. It was moved in 2013 to its current location after local residents requested it be replaced with a less ominous warning. It stands as a reminder of that horrific incident a half century ago.

In 1981, Ron Howard and Art Carney starred in the TV movie *Bitter Harvest* that was based on the tragic event.

The Barn in Bridgeport

Location:
6190 Dixie Hwy.
Bridgeport, MI 48722

The Bridgeport Historical Village is located in Bridgeport a few miles west of I-75. It has a group of buildings, including an old town hall, firehouse, schoolhouse and a chapel. One of the buildings is an old barn. It was built north of Bay City in Kawkawlin between 1881 and 1885 by Henry Jones on a land grant signed by President Ulysses S. Grant. The farm passed to the Hartley family in the early 1900s and was used until the 1960s when the Bridgeport Players acquired the barn from Charles Hartley to use as a community theater and dance hall. The barn was disassembled and moved to its current location in 1975, where it was reassembled and restored. It is now maintained by the Bridgeport Historical Society and is used to display antique farming equipment donated by local farmers.

Sit Down Strike

Location:
Sitdowners Memorial Park
1901 Executive Plaza Dr.
Flint, MI 48507

A few blocks northeast of the Flint Truck and Bus assembly plant is a small park with a memorial to the Sit Down Strike. After the Great Depression, the Wagner Act was created in 1935, guaranteeing workers the right to organize and join labor unions and to engage in collective bargaining and strikes. Before that, companies would ruthlessly stop workers from unionizing by firing them or threatening them with violence. In 1932, a protest at Ford was broken up by police and became a riot that left four workers dead.

On December 30, 1936, the workers at General Motors Fisher Body Plant stopped production and barricaded themselves inside the plant. They learned the company was going to move the dies that stamp out most of the body parts for GM's cars. Rather than picketing outside, they occupied the plant so GM could not move the stamping dies or bring in scab workers to break the union strike. The workers welded the doors shut and covered the windows with car body parts. Confined to the plant and living there for the foreseeable future, they slept on piled-up car mats and makeshift beds out of car seats. Local grocery stores, farmers and families donated food. Outside the plant, women raised funds to take care of the workers' families and even formed human shields to fend off police.

Without the body parts, most of General Motors production came to a halt. GM tried to stop the strike in the courts, and even received an injunction that said the workers were trespassing.

GM had the law on their side, but most of the public empathized with the workers. Two weeks after the strike began, GM cut off heat in 16-degree weather. When workers went outside to complain, security guards and police stormed the plant with tear gas. Workers fought back, throwing everything from automobile bolts to pieces of roof on the attackers before the police finally fled. Workers called the fight the "Battle of the Running Bulls".

Governor Murphy sent in the Michigan National Guard, not to help one side or the other, but to keep the peace. After 44 days, the United Auto Workers of America and GM came to an agreement and production resumed.

The Communal Cup

Location:
606 E Genesee.
Saginaw, MI 48607

In front of the police department in downtown Saginaw is a stone fountain. It stands in a small park dedicated to early Saginaw pioneer Michael Jeffers. After his death, his brother and niece donated land and money for a park.

The popularity of drinking fountains in America grew in the late 1800s. These fountains not only provided fresh water for people but also for dogs and horses.

It was decided that a drinking fountain for the citizens of Saginaw was needed. This beautiful fountain with a bust of Jeffers on the top and lion heads spewing water out of their mouths was built. It was dedicated in 1906. The water came from a well that was drilled below. There was also a space where ice could be placed around pipes to cool the water. People could drink from cups connected to the fountain with chains. It was not until 1915 that the health department decided it was not a good idea to have thousands of people sharing and drinking from the same cup, and they were removed from the fountain. Today the fountain has been restored and water still flows from the lions' heads in the summer months, although I would not drink from it.

Around the corner from the fountain is the Castle Museum. It was a former US Post Office that has been converted into a history museum.

Pioneer Log Village

Location:
205 S Hanselman St.
Bad Axe, MI 48413

The Town of Bad Axe is located in the heart of Michigan's Thumb. In the city park is a collection of six historic log cabin buildings that make up the Pioneer Village. The pioneer home, general store, one room school, chapel, barn and a blacksmith shop were all built between 1875 and the 1900s, and moved from their original locations around Huron County. They are maintained by the Huron County Historical Society and filled with artifacts to reflect the time period they are from.

It is interesting to see a log cabin church and school; it is like stepping back in time visiting them. The old log cabin house belonged to Mr. and Mrs. George Ullrich. It was built in one day with the help of the community. The modest home is twenty by thirty feet, and it is remarkable because they raised their eleven children in this six hundred square foot home. It seems humorous by today's standard family home, when people can't live without walk-in closets and a two car garage.

The town of Bad Axe got its name sometime around 1865 when a military surveyor, Captain Rudolph Papst, named a campsite at the meeting of two major trails "Bad Axe Camp" on his charts. He supposedly saw an old rusted ax left at the campsite by local hunters. It was incorporated as the village of Bad Axe on March 19,

1885; the name still stands today. An old ax-head, embedded in a small section of a tree and believed possibly to be the original camp ax, is on display at the Bad Axe Library.

The village is open Sunday afternoons from 2-4 pm during the summer months between Memorial Day Weekend and Labor Day. Admission is free, but donations are welcomed.

Pump House

Location:
2282 Ottawa Beach Rd.
Holland, MI 49424

If you have ever been to the beach at Holland State Park, you have probably been past this old brick building that stands along Ottawa Beach Road. It was built in 1901 as an Edison Electric Power Plant to provide lighting for the Ottawa Beach Hotel complex.

Sadly, the hotel burned down in 1923, and pumps were installed in the old powerhouse to supply water to the surrounding cottages. The "pump house" was used until the 1980s but was decommissioned when the municipal water supply came in from Holland. More recently the pumphouse has been converted into a local museum by the Historic Ottawa Beach Society.

The museum is on the Black Lake Boardwalk that links the Mt. Pisgah Dune Stairs to Lake Michigan Beach at Holland State Park. It is a great place to take a stroll and get away from the crowds at the beach, and there are a couple of wonderful ice cream shops nearby to stop for a cool treat. Or the other way around: stop for some ice cream and then check out the museum to learn a little bit of the history of the area.

> Holland State Park Beach is one of the most popular beaches in Michigan. If you go on a hot day, be sure to get there early because it will be busy and they close the entrance when the parking lot gets full.

Chapter Three
Northern Lower Peninsula

A Tombstone in the Woods

Location:
Near intersection of Mayfield and
Knight Roads northeast of Kingsley
44.6266061, -85.450260

A lonely tombstone stands in the northern Michigan woods near Kingsley. Not far from the ORV trail, it is strange to see a solitary headstone among the ferns in the tall trees. It is for Emma L. Northrup, who died while traveling with her parents. Her family was traveling by horse and buggy in 1875 from New York to Michigan to start a new life farming when 6-year-old Emma became ill and died. They laid her body to rest along the trail. A new marker replaced the older one and is located near Mayfield and Knight Roads. When I visited, there were many trinkets left at little Emma's grave. Because it is near an ORV trail, many riders stop at the grave to pay their respects to the little girl laid to rest in the woods.

The road to the grave is a seasonal forest road. It is passable with a passenger car, but I would recommend a four wheel drive SUV or truck because it is sandy in a few spots. If you are going to drive to it, I would do it in the summer months because the roads are not plowed in the winter.

Treat's Farm

Location:
13351 Norconk Rd.
Honor, MI 49640
44.79301, -86.0579

South of Empire where Norconk Road makes a sharp
bend about a mile west of M-22 is the Treat Farm Trail.
The trail is not posted, but it is part of Sleeping Bear
Dunes National Lakeshore. You will find an old farm
along the trail. It is not abandoned but maintained by the
National Park Service.

74

The farm was originally started in the 1840s by John Tweddle. After living in a log cabin on the property for decades, he built the current farm house in the 1880s. In 1912, Charles Treat and his wife, Martha, bought the farm and raised their family on the remote countryside along Lake Michigan. The barn on the property was purchased near Detroit by Charles, and he had it disassembled and shipped by rail to Empire. The pieces were transported by horses to the farm and reassembled.

Charles Treat's education was in engineering, and he used his knowledge on his farm. The house did not have running water. He tried drilling a well, but it kept getting plugged up with sand. He set up a set of eve troughs on the house to collect rainwater in a cistern for the house. He also experimented with concrete, making a root cellar in the side of the hill and a unique concrete domed garage. Eventually, the property became part of Sleeping Bear Dunes and is open to hikers to explore. A trail next to the barn leads up to a bluff overlooking Lake Michigan with spectacular views of the dunes and the blue water of Lake Michigan.

The trail does not have a parking lot so most people park along Norconk Road.

Jacktown

Location:
County Line Rd
Honor, MI 49640
44.778861, -85.98759

In the woods west of Garey Lake in the Leelanau
Peninsula on County Line road is an old cemetery. The
largest headstone has the name Bland chiseled on it, and
therefore, it is named Bland Cemetery. It is also shown on

77

some maps as the Jacktown Cemetery and is what remains of the old railroad town.

The town was built along the tracks of the Empire and Southeastern Railroad nicknamed the Empire Slow and Easy. It is rumored the town died off after the well went dry, but more likely it disappeared after the railroad went out of business and the tracks were removed in the 1920s. As far as I could tell, nothing remains of Jacktown but Bland Cemetery. If you visit the Leelanau Peninsula and you want to get away from the tourists and you like old cemeteries, be sure to check out the Bland Cemetery.

Negwegon Spring

Location:
Negwegon State Park Rd.
Ossineke, MI 49766
44.85568, -83.32480

Negwegon State Park is over 4000 acres of wilderness located along Lake Huron between Alpena and Harrisville. It was created in the 1960s and originally named Alpena State Park. Conservationist, and Alpena resident C. Hazlett Kramer lobbied to have the name of the park changed to Negwegon for the Ojibwe chieftain who hunted in the region. It is a popular park with hikers and birders. The park also has seven miles of Lake Huron shoreline. Most of it is a beautiful sandy beach, and if you are looking for a secluded place to relax on a hot day, Negwegon is a great place for it. A natural artesian spring is located on the trail between the parking lot and the beach. If you visit this out of the way park, be sure to bring a few water bottles to fill up with the crystal clear water.

Be careful when driving to Negwegon State Park; the road that leads to the park is Sand Hill Trail, and it is a narrow and sandy forest road winding through the trees.

Kraitz Cabin

Location:
S. Bohemian Rd.
Maple City, MI 49664
44.910754, -85.8778201

In the Leelanau Peninsula not far from M-22 near School Lake is a little log cabin. It was constructed by Francis Kraitz around 1856. He came to the area to escape the typhoid epidemic sweeping through Chicago. The cabin was originally built further south near St. Joseph Catholic Church. In 1945, John Kraitz (3rd generation) moved the house to a site beside School Lake, and just a few years later, he moved it across the road to its current location. The park service took ownership of the cabin in 2013. It had a few additions added on to it over the years, including green siding. It has recently been restored to its original construction. I am not sure what the plans are for the future of the cabin, but it sure looks peaceful surrounded by the northern Michigan forest.

The Jail And The Cabin

Location:
404 S Huron St.
Cheboygan, MI 49721

A few blocks south of downtown Cheboygan is an old building with the words COUNTY JAIL chiseled in the block above the door. It was built in 1880 and served as the Cheboygan County sheriff's residence and jail until 1969. In the late 1800s, many drunken and rowdy lumbermen sobered up in the jail. The inmates often did chores in exchange for their bed and meals prepared by the sheriff's wife.

By 1911, the jail was inadequate and a two-story addition was added to the original building. It was supposed to have 8 cells on each floor, but due to safety regulations, the second floor was never finished. The county used the jail until 1969 when a new modern jail was built to replace it. In 1972, the building became a museum maintained by the Historical Society of Cheboygan County.

Behind the old jail in Cheboygan is an old log cabin. At one time it stood near Burt Lake in the town of Indianville. It was relocated in the 1970s to its current spot and stands as a reminder of a tragic day in Michigan history.

On October 15, 1900, the sheriff came from Cheboygan to Indian Village, located on Indian Point on Burt Lake. John Walter McGinn purchased the land for back taxes of which the Native Americans did not owe because the land was given to them in a treaty with the government. When the men in the village were out of town working, the women and children were forcibly removed from their homes and then their houses burned to the ground by the sheriff and his men. The former residents of the burned town moved to other Indian villages, including Cross Village and the town of Indianville, where this old log cabin once stood. Sadly, few people know the story of the Burt Lake Burnout.

> The Cheboiganing Band St. Mary Cemetery stands alongside lakeshore cabins on Burt Lake where the village once stood. It is located at 10233 Chickagami Trail, Brutus, MI 49716.

Sears House

Location:
Hoeft State Park
5001 US-23
Rogers City, MI 49779

Near the shores of Lake Huron in Hoeft State Park is a
pleasant little house that is available for visitors to rent.
This is no ordinary house since it is a historic Sears mail-
order kit house. Built by park rangers and the Civilian

Conservation Corps in 1929, it was erected on the road that leads into the campground. The model was the Sears-Roebuck Rodessa, but the floor plan was modified by the builders so the house could accommodate two rangers' families if needed. The house has three bedrooms and sleeps up to eight people. It includes a sunroom, game room, and master bedroom with an attached bathroom. Sears catalog homes were catalog and kit houses sold primarily through mail order by Sears, Roebuck and Company. Sears reported that more than 70,000 of these homes were sold in North America between 1908 and 1940. More than 370 home designs in a wide range of architectural styles and sizes were offered over the program's 33-year history.

If you're looking for a house to stay at in northern Michigan, check out the lodge at Hoeft State Park. Next time you are at Hoeft and drive past it going to the campground, you will know a little bit about this magnificent little lodge.

Leland Jail

Location:
127 Chandler St.
Leland, MI 49654

The town of Leland in the Leelanau Peninsula is known for its historic Fishtown. It draws many tourists to the seaside village, but few of them know about this old brick building that stands near the center of town. The bars on the windows give a clue about what it was used for. In the

88

early days of the county, it served as the jail. I am sure it has held many people, but one person in particular made this little building world famous in the early 1900s.

Sister Janina, a nun in the small town of Isadore, went missing. Years later, her remains were found under the church, and the local law enforcement believed the priest's housekeeper Stanislawa "Stella" Lipczynska committed her murder. She was held in this old brick jail while the prosecutors built their case.

Stanislawa "Stella" Lipczynska standing
in the doorway of the Leleand jail

The trial garnered national attention as people read about the case in newspapers. Lipczynska was found guilty of murdering Sister Janina because she was jealous of the affair between the church's priest, Father Andrew, and the nun. When Sister Janina's body was found, it was discovered that the nun had been pregnant. Lipczynska denied having any involvement in the nun's death until the day she died. Exactly what happened will never be known.

For the whole story, I recommend reading *Isadore's Secret* by Mardi Link. It is interesting not only for the murder, but understanding the lives and history of people living in the Leelanau Peninsula at the turn of the century.

The Other Grand Hotel

Location:
8567 Portage Point Dr.
Onekama, MI 49675

On the shores of Portage Lake near Onekama is a large resort. The historic complex of buildings are the Portage Point Resort. It is reminiscent of the Grand Hotel on Mackinac Island because it was constructed by the same builder of the Grand Hotel. The Portage Point Resort was built in 1902, and about ten years after it was

91

constructed, the canal from Lake Michigan to Portage Lake was dredged. Large steamships could bring guests from Chicago and Milwaukee to relax in northwestern Michigan. Over the decades, the resort has maintained its unique historic look.

Driving the road past the Portage Point Resort to Lake Michigan, you will find Captain John Langland Park. It has a beautiful sandy beach on Lake Michigan and is a great place on a sunny summer day for a swim or to lay out and work on your tan. The park is named for John Langland, the lighthouse keeper that tended the light at the end of the pier. A kerosene light tower was built in 1891, and Langland tended the light until 1917. Today a steel tower with an automated electrical lamp guides boaters into the canal, but the park honors the man who lit the old lamp.

A Strange Boat in the Park

Location:
410 E Main St.
Harbor Springs, MI 49740

In the resort town of Harbor Springs is a strange looking long and narrow dark blue boat on display in the park. It was named the *Aha* and built by inventor Ephraim Shay, who lived in Harbor Springs. His house still stands across the road from the park and is a National Historic Site. The boat was designed and built by Shay at his machine

93

Th *Aha* abandoned at Wilderness State Park.

shop. Its long and narrow hull made it one of the fastest boats at the time.

While being towed to storage in the 1930s, the empty hull of the *Aha* took on water and was beached near Sucker Creek in the present day Wilderness State Park. The old boat sat there for decades, slowly rusting and being used for target practice by hunters.

In 2003, the hull was brought back to Harbor Springs where it sat in storage. In 2019, it was trucked to Onaway and restored by the students at the Industrial Arts Institute. After restoring and repainting the hull, the *Aha* was put on display at the park in the town where it was built.

High Accuracy Mark

Location:
5401 Monument Rd.
Oscoda, MI 48750

Lumberman's Monument along the Au Sable River near Oscoda receives thousands of visitors every year. It was built in 1931 and managed by the United States Forest Service. At the heart of the monument is a fourteen-foot tall bronze sculpture depicting a lumber cruiser, sawyer, and river rat. The cruiser surveyed the forests for timber, the sayer cut down the trees and the river rat guided the logs down the river to the sawmill.

Behind the monument is an overlook with a spectacular view of the Au Sable River. The grounds also have lumbering era artifacts on display along with a visitor center that was built by the Civilian Conservation Corps.

One item along the path is a metal disk. It looks like a manhole cover, but it is an important location in the United States. It was placed in 2005 as part of the U.S. Forest Service's Century of Service Celebration and is one of sixteen highly accurate survey markers placed around America for precise location. I wonder how many people walk past this unassuming marker and don't know what it is.

Benchmarks are round disks about four inches in diameter. They are placed on the ground and used by surveyors. I have spotted them at several important landmarks such as lighthouses, bridges and government buildings. Next time you are out exploring an old historic place, keep an eye out for one of these survey marks.

Ghost Town of Stratford

Location:
11101 N 13 Mile Rd
Lake City, MI 49651
44.495569, -84.952857

About five miles west of Higgins Lake along N. 13 Mile Road is a wooden sign for the long gone town of Stratford. The town started in 1897 when the Thayer Lumber Company purchased 13,400 acres of virgin red and white pine. The railroad laid tracks to the lumber town and hauled the logs out for twelve years. The population of Stratford grew to about 1200 people and had a hotel, general store and several saloons for the lumberjacks to spend their hard earned money.

By 1908, the surrounding trees were gone, and the workers and citizens had abandoned the town. The region was purchased by the state in 1937. Nothing remains of the town but memories and signs placed to mark the location of some of the buildings. It is interesting to wander around and look at the signs with the names of different buildings and imagine what it was like more than a century ago.

Down the road about a quarter mile is an ORV/snowmobile trailhead and parking lot. The old townsite is a great place to stop next time you are out for a ride.

A Campsite with a Grave

Location:
Ossineke State Forest Campground
Ossineke, MI 49766
44.92058, -83.41220

Michigan has thousands of campsites in parks, forests and campgrounds all across the state for people to enjoy the great outdoors. Campsite Number 4 at the Ossineke State Forest Campground, south of Alpena, is unique. It is a beautiful campsite overlooking Lake Huron, but it also has a strange and interesting distinction. Next to it is a stone marker for the gravesite of A.J. Michalowski—Born 3-16-1839, Died 11-6-1865.

He was buried where his headstone now stands after his body was washed ashore. He worked at the Oliver Sawmill in Ossineke, and in November 1865, he sailed a small boat across Thunder Bay to Alpena. Unfortunately, he never made it to his destination.

I thought it was strange that he was never buried in a cemetery. I could not find more information, but I can only assume he capsized in a storm. His body came ashore later and was in a highly decomposed state, so it was immediately buried.

The Frame at Waugoshance Point

Location:
End of Wilderness State Park Drive.
Take the hiking trail straight out the
point for about a mile to see the
frame.
Approximately 45.756286, -84.979825

Waugoshance Point sits out at the far western end of
Wilderness State Park at the tip of the mitten. A
mysterious resting metal framework rests on the point. It

is about 5 feet tall, 10 feet long and about 3 feet wide. The tubing at the back has been cut off so it may have been a lot longer at one time. I have seen where some people refer to it as a glider frame. After looking at it, I am not convinced that is what it is. I did not have a magnet with me, but I am sure it is made out of thin wall steel tubing. The fact that it is steel makes me think that it was not used for anything aeronautical since it would be rather heavy. It does look like it may have been used by the military since it seems rather complicated in design. Some people have said it looks like an old dune buggy frame, but that does not look right to me either.

During World War II, the U.S. Navy did some top secret drone testing in northern Lake Michigan and used the old Waugoshance Lighthouse for a target. The drones of WWII were not like the modern drones of today. They were small airplanes with a wingspan of about six feet. They were radio controlled by another airplane that flew alongside it. Some were even equipped with a video camera, and an operator could watch on a monitor.

I am thinking that the strange metal framework could be some part of the launching mechanism for a drone, but I am still not sure about that. I looked all over it for a serial number or some sort of markings, but I could not find anything. It is about a quarter mile hike from the end of the Wilderness State Park Drive to the framework. But also be aware that it may be surrounded by water if the lake levels are high.

Chapter Four
Upper Peninsula

Irish Hollow Cemetery

Location:
Rockland Rd./ US-45
southeast of Rockland
46.7305288, -89.1675303

Rockland is located in the western Upper Peninsula. The town was an old mining town where several Irish immigrants came to work in the mines. Southeast of town off US-45 is the Irish Hollow Cemetery. It sits in the woods, and the tombstones are surrounded by tall grass and ferns. It may be a little overgrown, but it is a beautiful old cemetery.

According to a local legend, the cemetery was dedicated on July 4th, 1892. A little girl from town ran up to the ceremony to tell the people the town was on fire. Her parents had let her stay home instead of going to the dedication. She said she found a firecracker and lit it in her home. When she threw it out the window, it caught the curtain on fire and spread through the town. The townspeople raced back to Rockland, but the fire had destroyed a large portion of the town.

After the mines closed in the early 1900s, the population of the town declined, and about two hundred residents live there today. If you go through town and you like old cemeteries, be sure to check out the Irish Hollow Cemetery.

About three miles southwest of Rockland is the Old Victoria Historic Townsite. It is a restoration of an old mining town and has several log buildings for visitors to explore.

Bay Furnace

Location:
Bay Furnace Campground
E7900 W, M-28
Munising, MI 49862

Bay Furnace Campground is a National Forest campground that sits west of Christmas off M-28. You will want to visit this campground, even if you don't camp, because you will find the ruins of an old iron smelting furnace that gives the campground its name. The entrance is across from the casino. Before the driveway enters the campground is a parking lot that has a short. trail that leads to the ruins.

The location was originally a Native American fishing village named Onota, and its name means "the place where fishermen live". In 1869, the Bay Furnace Company built the blast furnace along the shores of Lake Superior. Grand Island made for a natural harbor, and the surrounding forests supplied firewood for the furnace. Men came to the area to work smelting iron ore into iron bars, and the town quickly grew in population. A church was built but did not have a pastor. Fr. Eis would walk one hundred miles round trip along stage roads to minister to the townspeople.

In 1877, a fire raced through the forests and Onota, and burned for three days, destroying most of the town. It is believed that hot ash from the furnace hauled away by wagon started the blaze. The Bay Furnace Company went bankrupt and never rebuilt the furnace. Another town

111

nearby took the name Onoda. The area became known as Christmas because in 1938, Julius Thorson built a holiday toy factory in the area. Sadly, the toy factory burned down two years later, but the name stuck.

The ruins of the old furnace still stand along the shoreline. They have been crumbling over the decades, and in the 1990s, the Forest Service added some timbers to stabilize them. If you are passing through the area, be sure to stop and check out the old furnace. It also has a great view of Lake Superior. If you look closely, you can see some of the timbers used for a dock stretched out into the lake for the steamships to load and unload at the furnace.

A few miles east of the casino is the Grand Island Harbor Rear Range Lighthouse hidden in the trees. Look for the path next to the "Welcome to Christmas" sign on M-28 for a path to the light tower.

The Big Steam Engine

Location:
Trout Creek Twp. Park
102 Pine St,
Trout Creek, MI 49967

The town of Trout Creek is on the western side of the Upper Peninsula. M-28 crosses over a creek of the same name; it's how the town got its name. Abbott Fox Community Park is located on M-28 and has an old mill pond that was created on the creek. In the park you will see a massive old steam engine. The mechanical monster was made in 1912 by Allis Chalmers and was originally used in a Minneapolis Minnesota flour mill.

In 1921, it was moved to Trout Creek and used in the Weidman Lumber Company's sawmill until 1968. The sawmill no longer stands, but the steam engine sits on display as a reminder of a time in the Upper Peninsula when steam powered factories and sawmills. The flywheel is sixteen feet in diameter and photos do not convey the massive size of this old steam engine. Next time you are traveling along M-28, be sure to stop and check out this historic steam engine.

Sac Bay

Location:
Sac Bay County Park
End of 8th Rd.
Garden, MI 49835
45.656536, -86.7038923

Sac Bay is near the tip of the Garden Peninsula between Fayette and Fairport. It is a small bay on the shores of Big Bay De Noc and was named by the French for a band of indigenous Saulk people who lived there. A town by the same name was started in 1853. It was given a post office

115

in 1860, but it closed after a post office was opened in Fayette. An old building stands across from an old farm where the town once stood. It looks as if it was a general store at one time and then it had a metal addition added to it.

At the end of 8th Street is a small county park with a beach on Lake Michigan. It is a beautiful and quiet park with picnic tables and grills. If you are looking for a secluded place to enjoy a picnic or sit on the beach, be sure to check out this little county park.

M-107

Location:
M-107 along Lake Superior near the
entrance of Porcupine Mt. State Park
Roadside Park at
46.819021, -89.634293

If you visit the Lake of the Clouds in Porcupine
Mountains Wilderness State Park, you need to drive down
M-107 to the lake. It is about a ten-mile stretch of road
that travels along the shoreline of Lake Superior. You will

probably notice a sign and a couple of boulders dedicating the road as the 107th Engineer Memorial Highway.

When the roadway was built in 1935, it was named to honor the 107th Engineer Combat Battalion. The battalion is a large unit of the Michigan Army National Guard stationed in Ishpeming, Michigan, and it traces its history to the Michigan State Troops, which was the predecessor organization to the Michigan National Guard. The 107th Engineer Battalion is even connected to the Calumet Light Guard that was formed in 1881.

During WWII, the unit built the longest tactical floating bridge in the world across the Rhine. The 1370-foot-long bridge was built in 14 hours and nicknamed 'Victor Bridge' by the troops. The unit has also been activated for State Emergencies such as the 1967 Detroit Riots, the 1976 Great Seney Fire and several snowstorms in the Upper Peninsula. In the summer of 2016 they were called into active duty and assisted in repairing roads in the Keweenaw that were washed away in a heavy rainstorm.

In 2001, the Michigan Legislature officially named it the "107th Engineer Memorial Road". The unit's motto is "Good as Done!" Next time you visit the Porkies and are traveling down M-107, I hope you will remember that it is more than just a number for a road, but that it honors the men and women from the Upper Peninsula engineer combat battalion who have continued to serve the state and the country for more than a century.

The Log Cabin

Location:
Manistique Historical Park
121 Deer St.
Manistique, MI 49854

The Alva Kepler log cabin sits in Manistique's Pioneer
Park next to the water tower. The rustic house dates back
to the 1880s and was once part of the Byers' settlement in

Hiawatha Township, located about twelve miles north of Manistique. The cabin was part of the cooperative community known as the "Hiawatha Village Association". It was formed in the 1890s when Abe Byers convinced people who were struggling from an economic depression at the time to form a commune and combine their assets. About two hundred people agreed to turn over their homes and property to the community and live in the village. They had about 225 residents the first year and grew crops and made goods to sell in Milwaukee.

After the first year they were not successful because they had difficulty selling their crops and the cost to ship the products they made were more than they could sell them for. When Alva Kepler and his brother John were supposed to move into the village the following year, they sued to withdraw from the community. Shortly afterwards, many other people sued, and the homes and items were split up among the members, ending the short-lived experiment. Eventually the cabin was moved to Pioneer Park and restored. It stands today as a reminder of a well-meaning experimental community that ultimately failed.

Standing near the Kepler cabin in Pioneer Park is a historic water tower that is probably one of the country's most beautiful water towers. It also has some of the city's old fire engines, including a 1914 Dodge Brothers truck and attached 1880s hook and ladder trailer.

St Peter the Fisherman Cemetery

Location:
4473 II Ln,
Garden, MI 49835

South of the historic Fayette townsite is an old cemetery on the shoreline of Lake Michigan. A sign next to the road denotes it as St. Peter the Fisherman Cemetery. It was the Catholic cemetery for Fayette, and a Protestant cemetery was north of town. A short trail from the road leads to the cemetery hidden in the trees.

It is a beautiful little cemetery with old headstones and newer wooden crosses. One of the earliest burials was in 1877. The one thing that stood out to me was the metal fencing surrounding a couple of burial plots. It was strange how it was all mangled and twisted as if some supernatural force had hit it. I am thinking a tree fell on it or maybe ice from a storm, but for whatever reason, it looked odd. If you like old cemeteries and you are visiting Fayette, be sure to check out the old cemetery. It is near the Port Bar & Family Restaurant.

Halliwell

Location:
Off S. Boundary Rd. In the
Porcupine Mountains State Park
about two miles south of the visitors
center near the Union Mine.

The remnants of the old Halliwell mine can be found in the Porcupine Mountains Wilderness State Park. Constructed in 1895, the mine once stood south of the visitor's center on S. Boundary Road. The mine company sank two vertical shafts. but it never made a profit and closed in 1908.

After the mine closed, things got a little interesting. Two brothers, George and Gus Biggie, lived at the mine. They were born in the Porkies in the 1890s. They attended school at the nearby ghost town of Nonesuch where their father ran a general store. They lived in the old office of the mine and raised chickens, grew a garden and guided hunters and tourists as a way to make some extra money.

When the state of Michigan took over the land to create the state park, George and Gus were given special permission to live at the old mine. After they both passed away in the 1970s, the mine structures were removed. Only a few remnants of the mine remain along with a fenced off hole where the shaft was sunk into the earth. Visitors to the park can stop at a parking lot on S. Boundary Road and see traces of the old mine.

Not far away from the Halliwell mine site is the former town of Nonesuch where you can still see the mine entrance and some of the stone walls of the old buildings.

Little Girls Point

Location:
E1930 Lake Rd.
Ironwood, MI 49938

Along the shoreline of Lake Superior west of Ironwood and not far from the Wisconsin border is Little Girls Point. It is a county park and a beautiful place to stop for a picnic and watch the waves on Lake Superior or the sunset at the end of the day.

126

The name of the park is a curious one, and it has a unique story. Legend has it that a young Chippewa woman named Leelinaw lived with her family further to the north in what is now the Porcupine Mountains State Park. She loved to paddle her canoe along the shoreline of the great lake they call Gitche Gumee (Lake Superior). She was told not to stop at the point covered in pine trees because it was haunted by Puk Wadginees or "the little men of the wood".

On the day of her wedding, Leelinaw ventured out as she had done before and stopped at the point to explore the grove of pine trees. She never returned, and as the day turned into night, the point was searched using torches, but Leelinaw was never found. A wooden sign stands in the park telling the story of Leelinaw and her disappearance.

Not far from the park is Superior Falls located on the Montreal River that makes up the border between Michigan and Wisconsin.

Ontonagon Poor Farm

Location:
18754 M-38
Ontonagon, MI 49953
(privately owned, please do not
trespass)

A few miles east of Ontonagon on M-38 is a massive old
building covered up by trees and bushes. The dilapidated
structure was part of the Ontonagon County Poor Farm.

The county's first poor farm was constructed in 1855 to help take care of lumberjacks and people in need of assistance. The home also cared for people with physical and mental disabilities as well as chronic illnesses such as tuberculosis. Inmates came from all over the Upper Peninsula, and according to old records, their cause of poverty was usually due to mental or physical illness.

Ontonagon Poor Farm circa 1900

The building that stands today was built in 1900 on a 200 acre farm. The people who lived at the home and were able to work grew crops and raised livestock until the facility closed in 1946 and the residents moved to a facility in Gibb City. The old building now sits on a privately owned cattle farm. Please be respectful and do not trespass. The building is not open to the public, but it is visible from the road.

The Ontonagon County Historical Society has a wonderful museum in downtown Ontonagon on River Street. Here you can get tickets to tour the Ontonagon lighthouse.

Jackson Mine

Location:
Jackson Mine Park
199 Tobin St
Negaunee, MI 49866
Mine opening near
46.49832837, -87.6228258

Southwest of downtown Negaunee, you will find several old staircases built in the berms and hills that lead to nowhere. This region of the city is known as Old Town, and at one time it had several houses and buildings. They

131

are all gone now, and only the foundations and concrete stairs remain. The area had all the buildings because of the Jackson Mine which was located nearby. The mine was the first iron ore mine in the Lake Superior region. In 1844, surveyor William Burt noticed some strange fluctuations on his compass, and upon further investigations he noticed iron ore deposits. Soon afterwards, the first mine was dug.

The mine closed in the 1940s, and by the 1950s, several structures in the area had collapsed due to shafts underneath caving in. Because of the unstable grounds, the buildings in Old Town were either moved or demolished. It is now part of a park that the Heritage Trail passes through. You can still drive down the old streets and see several staircases that once led to homes in Old Town. Today there is a fenced off opening in the side of a cliff that leads into the mine. Visitors can take a short trail to the opening from the Iron Ore Heritage Trail parking lot. The parking lot also has several mining artifacts on display.

The historic Old Town Negaunee region has been converted into a park with a disc golf course.

Boot Hill Cemetery

Location:
Old Seney Rd.
South of Seney
46.3392284, -85.942105

South of the town of Seney in the Upper Peninsula on Old Seney Road (County Road 456) is the old Boot Hill Cemetery. Most of the graves are marked with simple wooden crosses. They do not give names or dates, only a reminder that someone is laid to rest in the old cemetery. They are early Yoopers who worked and lived around Seney long before trucks and snowmobiles. It is said that some of the men buried in the cemetery are early lumberjacks from a time when the rowdy men came into Seney in the late 1880s to spend their hard earned money on liquor and gambling. I can't imagine how challenging life was for them a few centuries ago.

The cemetery has a more modern section, but if you head into the trees at the northern part, you will see some of the old wooden grave markers.

Haight Township Hall

Location:
9040 US-45.
Bruce Crossing, MI 49912

Along US-45 north of Paulding is a beautiful two-story yellow building with white trim and porch railings. It looks like something from a movie set or a historical park.

The sign at the top reads "Town Hall 1904". Still in use today, it is Haight Township Hall and serves the small township with a population of just over two hundred people. Traveling around Michigan, I come across a lot of small rural township halls and offices. Most are ordinary-looking buildings, and some are former schoolhouses. The hall in Haight Township on the west side of the UP is magnificent, and I am sure its citizens are proud of it.

The Rock Cut

Location:
Off Peshekee / Huron Bay Grade
road in the Huron Mountains
46.738832422255, -88.1727329522

Deep in the forests of the Huron Mountains in the northwest Upper Peninsula is a huge gash in the solid rock terrain. It was created in the 1890s to run the Iron Range and Huron Bay Railroad from Champion to an ore dock near Skanee on the Huron Bay in Lake Superior. A group of investors in the Detroit area thought they could make a fortune on hauling iron ore by train from a mine near Champion on Lake Michigamme. They spent about two million dollars and employed 1500 men building a railroad and ore dock.

The ore dock was massive. It was a thousand feet long and used over a million board feet of lumber in its construction. The railroad was about forty miles long and had to cut through the rugged and hilly terrain of the Huron Mountains. The most challenging part was cutting through a granite outcropping near Mount Arvon, the highest point in Michigan. It took three years and several lives to cut through the rock. Besides the dangers of blasting with black powder, several men contracted typhoid, and living in cramped quarters in a camp, the disease spread throughout the labor force.

Photo taken during construction

By the time the railroad was completed, the mine had stopped producing iron ore and the railroad was no longer needed. After all the work, money and lives lost to create the railroad, it never hauled one car load of iron ore. The railroad was sold for about $100,000, and the tracks were removed and used downstate.

The Huron Bay Peshekee Grade Road from US-41 will take you near the famed rock cut. The road follows along the Peshekee River and is constructed using part of the old railroad grade. It is not a trip for the faint of heart. It is about 20 miles of rough road back into the wilderness. Although it was a challenging trip to the rock cut, it was one of the most impressive things I have seen in Michigan. I can only imagine what kind of hell the men endured to create it, and the deepest cut of all is that it was never utilized.

If you travel out to see the Rock Cut be prepared for a trip into the remote wilderness. Make sure you have plenty of gas in your vehicle and you might want to let someone know you are headed out to see it. If your vehicle breaks down, you most likely will not have cell service. It took me about an hour one way to reach the Rock Cut so plan on it taking some time traveling on the rough roads.

Conclusion

I am still exploring the Great Lakes State and searching places I have not visited. There are a lot of wonderful and interesting things to see. Michigan is a large state from Detroit to the Keweenaw in the Upper Peninsula, and there are still a lot of roads I have not driven down. I hope you will continue to follow my journey at www.lostinmichigan.net.

I have also been exploring other states, and you can follow my journey through them at www.lostinthestates.com.

Continue following
my journey at

www.lostinmichigan.net

To follow my travels outside of
Michigan you can visit

www.lostinthestates.com